the night watches

THE NIGHT WATCHES

Gary Metras

ADASTRA PRESS
1981

Some of these poems first appeared in the
following magazines: *Abbey, Bardic Echoes, Bezoar,
Contact II, In a Nutshell, Jump River Review, A
Letter Among Friends, Modus Operandi, Pikestaff
Forum, The Third Eye* and *Xanadu.*

ADASTRA PRESS
101 Strong Street
Easthampton, Mass.   01027

for my wife

Contents

II. STILL LIVES

III. THE OPENING ABSENCE

i. the watchers

. . . the history of poetry in all ages
is the attempt to find new images
for the moon.
——J. ISAACS,
THE BACKGROUND OF MODERN POETRY

For it is only our consciousness
that does not yet know; the unconscious
seems already informed.
——JUNG,
MAN AND HIS SYMBOLS

Moon Song I

We always sing of the moon
its light   its darkness

like habits in motion around us
urging with a gentle urge

the directions of dream
and the promises of love

We mapped its slightest inflections
walked among them

and still our green world
these tides of emotion

are a mystery

A Concise History of Pebbles

As sunlight gathered the gases
pebbles leaked small darknesses

When rain first washed the earth
pebbles dripped pent-up silences

For the winds came and pebbles
curled up to sleep

On moonless nights pebbles ebbed
deeper into themselves

and waited for man

Gothic

At the edge of the black silence of water
on this graceless night of no moon,
not even moths dare stir.
The fires go out one by one.
Stars keep their distance between obscuring clouds
and hold no hope
for the mind trapped in a body
surrendered to the dark.
A slug crawls blindly through the muck
and doesn't dream.
If Aries rams through the tightening clouds
with the force of his sex,
things will change.
Perhaps the moon will storm
the mountain's shadow
like a king regaining his castle.
There will be no mercy shown.
Not that evil slinks between the trees,
or waits at the bottom of the well for
the unsuspecting maiden,
or flies as silent as clouds to darken
what joy there is —
the child with toy snug under the blanket,
the man and woman dancing in their room,
the nun with rosary draped over the race,
the slug crawling, tasting earth's harvest —
it's just that with each new blink

something else disappears.
Traffic sounds in the distance,
like a breeze under the breastbone.
A voice whispers —
Everything you've always suspected
is true, and night does
expose the pure. —
The arms are empty,
or they are full of another self asking —
Who will come to relight the fires?

The Air Angels Walk

There is a need to billow and glow,
be loose like a cloud
bound to laws only the night sees.
The world is always shaped
by night and day. One revolution
solves nothing. The feet
may as well be bedrock
or the flotsam of glaciers
for all they will ever know of the air
angels walk, unless, like that cloud,
nocturnal vapors mold expiring breath
with the unseen weight
of the body radiating outward,
beyond the grip of mountains
and easy laws made for the moment.
The baobab blooms only at night;
this is the exception; its own law.
That idly drifting cloud cannot
hold, but feel how freely starlight
breezes the sky-leaning eyes.

The Large and Small of It

*. . . who would have dreamed this
infinitely little too much?*
——ROBINSON JEFFERS

He didn't see the particles of solar dust
land where his feet touched the beach
but he marked the length of the flight

When the ripple flowed beyond his sight
the raindrop became the puddle
and the river
and the ocean

The hoard of snow descending around him
might as well have been one flake
falling again   and again

He sometimes asked,   What weight
has the Milky Way in rain   or snow

To answer all this the poet chipped from stones
the heavy roots of memory
and made of them two towers

one for dust   snow   rain

the other for little dreams outweighing stars

Song Heard in the Street

Who knows if the sound was that
of the dead light calling
——EDITH SITWELL

World, world time is almost all

yours. Though we barely see it, had rarely
seen it slither up to our crumbling walls,
it approaches none the less, approached then
slithered away dropping charred bones. Bones will
be the awfull ruins for the diggers in
the future to piece us together. They
will find the bones rotted without reason,

scattered from wholeness. Their nightmares will be
like the visions that exploded the skulls
of bomb squads who wandered the fallen brick
in search of living death. But we didn't
explode; we burned quietly like moss. You
dear seekers, should pluck hawk droppings from out
of the ancient fields of sleep and turn them

in dusk light to see us, alone with stilled
voices, lonely amid the incessant
ticking, cavernous in our deadly light,
awaiting stabbing echoes from sirens
that sounded only in dreams, always in
dreams. This outlasted the calcium. This
is the smirk that can't be wiped from our jaws.

This is why pulsing hammers couldn't carve
out the ribless heart of the loneliness.
This is when the cancers consumed us in
silence. And so, world, gravitating time
like a tomb, lightless in the need, songless
in need, your marrow flowed with black light from
our emptiness while all the time we sang

mutely. Hush! What is that sound?

The Hands of Lovers

The hands of lovers are no light thing.
When they lock together
you hear a vault door close on its assets.
The dark inside the vault
is a dream come true.
The lovers count what they have:
hands and other parts;
small change in the bottoms of pockets;
underwear that shall be nameless;
two horses grazing on a hillside;
cloud-glow like an omen in night;
not a single place to put a stone.
The body is what water wears
between whispered breathing.
At moonrise all this will change.

In Paris

(for Natalie)

Was it all just the air of that hotel room,
antiqued with the traffic of countless couples
who fled night under frayed sheets?

The gray morning light of Christmas day
leaked through mist to pierce
the glassed balcony doors, and settled

about your face like a veil.
Time flicked from progression, and for
a moment you were a too-human Madonna,

childless, sitting on the bed, the breakfast
bread crumbling down shoulders, breasts and lap.
The worn chair facing you cradled me.

I squinted the dimmed light into half
and still couldn't see what needed seeing.
We dressed then roamed a nameless garden,

light rain filling the honeymoon smiles, the silences.
Now more than anything I remember those bright
crumbs sparkling on your winter pale skin

like the gold offered by a foolish Magi.

Fever

We stand by the crib silent as the moon.
The child twists like a netted fish.
Toy bears stare from the wall shelf;
their eyes pure black and empty,
insensible to what isn't joy.
For now we slowly breathe time
to calm the pulses as we recite
the procedure of ice baths. Or else
the fever will break of itself
and melt the forced ice packing our hearts.
All that can be said is in my arm
tight around your shoulders
as we fight off the hollowness
growing in our eyes like those
in the head of a plastic Jesus.

Soothing

the rocking chair rocks
away the darkness

with baby cradled
in arms and rhythms

that soothe night to yawns
where mother returns

to dream all seems well

The Night Watch

"I'll sit and see if that small sailing cloud
Will hit or miss the moon."
——ROBERT FROST

The boards on the porch slump.
They have known enough of weather,
like the wood of old ships,
but are not yet ready for surrender.
Somewhere a farmer's wife will go and sit
to keep night watch with strick planks
such as these and forget the mortgage,
certain that whatever happens next
is no caprice of night and wind.
Hay, labor, soil, all worn,
anticipating what daylight brings
like tide abandoned shellfish.
But now everything is in the moon
beginning its descent once again
and that cloud in pursuit,
darkness chewing its trailing edge
in a fateful yaw.

For the watch-posted sailor,
for each one of us drifting in night,
the slightest quiver threatens with omen.
is an undertow awaiting the false step.
Familiar things lose shape:
acres of corn are just another dark horizon
like water, mountains, the tops of trees,
that tower asleep on the hill
like a mast bared of sail.
Whatever stirs in this black flow
crawls like jagged claws out of water,
whether moon, a lost cloud
or hands trying to calm in a lap.
Tonight someone will drown
in an ocean of empty shells.
And the boards will stay nailed to the porch,
persistent till the end,
like a raft adrift,
the last hope of land.

Moon Song II

Their arriving changes nothing

Still a captive of other forces
My influence is negligible

The light I send is not mine
This journey is not mine

Even the rock's slow granulation
is the work of others

Somewhere out here   long ago
I missed the chance of life

and ever since must scribe
this brief circle on darkness

ii. still lives

Life is not empty; if anything, it is too full.
But the various items of experience and the
values attaching to them seem to stand
all on a par with one another. In such a world,
it is true that nothing makes a difference.
This is not because we are confronted
by nothing, but because there are no
differences. In the dark all cats are black.
——PHILIP H. RHINELANDER,
IS MAN INCOMPREHENSIBLE TO MAN?

It is the philosopher's privilege to call upon
the artist to show that what he is about
is either good in itself or a means to good. It is
the artist's duty to reply: "Art is good
because it exalts to a state of ecstasy better
far than anything a benumbed moralist can
even guess at; so shut up."
——CLIVE BELL,
ART

Let us use poetry, a relatively limited
pursuit, as our prime example.
——MERRITT CLIFTON,
FREEDOM COMES FROM HUMAN BEINGS

Still Life

Death dark edges frame tonight
with a hue so deep the dappled stars

have no effect and the crescent moon
slices the crisp sky like an afterthought

The difference between hills and heaven
is just a silent shading of black

that blends to make the orchard's height
false and the cut cornfield less severe

This dark this calm this peace is perfect
to languish in forgetting all

and be this world licked with shadow
if only the child wouldn't scream

his sleep born anguish like a knife
that slashes the still with life

The Last Midwife

she sits her
wrinkles rocking with
the chair beside

an ancient worm
infested cradle empty
except of cobwebs

The Celebration

This is a celebration by candlelight.
The bride is alone as she enters the room.
She does not yet know she is a bride.
The darkness will marry her,
taking just her hand at first,
as it did her mother's, and hers before that.
As each new night spreads
to the last places of light,
the dark demands more of the bride.
Soon nothing will be hers alone.
Her best friend won't recognize her.
Mother will half-smile and say—
    I tried to warn you
    but the light of my words
    had gone out.
Her years are spent memorizing
the steps from room to room.
Then one night she will find a room
where a half-burnt candle struggles.
She will take it up in trembling hands,
its light dancing a lost echo in her eyes,
and announce—
    This was not the dream I had.
    I can carry my own light.
    Now is the celebration.

Self-Portrait by Lamplight

The lampshade stands rigid
against the dark
on its plastic
neo-classical base,
like some centurion
emitting the light of order
into the livingroom
vacant
except for him
sprawled on the couch
obsessively chewing that pen.

Night taps at the door
and empties the picture
window.

A moth circles
concentric within the lampshade,
a lone,
ecstatic prisoner.

He will rise,
blink off the light,
abandon moth to memory
and pace in black rooms knawing
old themes.

Awaiting the Birth

She does not tell,
this flowering behind locked doors
of sleep, this wife, in pre-dawn
where sleep and dream are
the only firmth,
she does not tell
of her womb full with patient baby,
her thoughts lost
in the ninth month rhythm of sleep
as she hugs the new sag in the mattress
and discounts mine as too familiar,
the same old years sagging beside her
in the sheets of hoping and straining
that have brought us, at last,
to the awful solitude of creation
where I am left
to gloat, to wonder, and worry
about what will come of that one
sweated summer night
when the worn mattress
wailed like a night-born insect
who lives its meager hours to mate
and die,
and now you, intent,
in this before-dawn symphony
of inner clocks, listen
for the fish-sway of birth,
having slept in what room of the world,
you will not tell.

Teaching the Baby to Dream

In the third month of your acquaintance
with the world of occasional sun,
you ceased to breathe one moonlit night.

Sleep broke around me in a silent reveille.
I hurried, half naked, adrenalin awake,
driven to your room by a dreamt scream.

Bits of moonlight hovered in the cracks
of the curtain, waiting to descend.
Muted by halted breath, I stared and felt

the gagged stillness lumped in the crib,
in your tongue-swollen throat.
In a piece of time unstuck from time,

I reached deep into your mouth
unfurled the darkness sprouting there
dug it out and slapped your back

before I breathed into your lungs,
and your limp body surged, and you again
tick-tocked in time, in sleep, in dream.

Bouquet

Son, once you were amazed with fingers
blossoming from your palm.
We mimicked you and your simple face

grew brighter as hands opened
and closed like pink flowers.
Wonderment arranged your crib

into a six-handed bouquet.
Two years of growth and we
wanted another blossom.

Two nights ago I took your mother
to the hospital and the seed
of your sister or brother to be

was bad, and will not add
to our vase. We wilt in such a drought
and wait for future rain.

8/12/74

How Sunset Affects Perspective

(for Jerrie)

From where you sit, perhaps the sun
dips into the ocean in spangles of light.
But here the sun has already slipped behind
mountains—in one quick motion it was
gone; now you see it, now you don't;
just the ruby echo licking what clouds
there are. It isn't magic any more.
There are those who explain this as readily
as the dreams we'll soon briefly live.
But what other truths does he need who cups
a thing in hands no one else feels.
The child still sees what the man does not.
Some watch their sky with computers;
they sleep with the knowledge of
a 15 billion year old universe.
And the August moon, just springing into view
to light the far edge of my oceanic earth
and 3-D reveal shadowed mountains
east of you, is yet a child, and we too young
a race to know it all.

Eclipse

last night you
said you were
leaving me

that you would lift
off my heart
like a shadow

this happens
once every
seven years

Lovers at the Beach

A MASS FOR TWO

Antiphon *a voice, ghostly*
"Water flows, stars shine, people make love."
————ISSAC BABEL, vanished in 1939.

Introit *the lovers appear, speaking in unison*
In saecula saeculorum water, stars, people;
The flow, the shine, the love—
For one night more, have mercy. Mercy.

Gospel *the man says*
Dominus vobiscum. According to Babel,
O waters, flow with us, engulf our bodies
In flaccid waves and baptize this love.
Gloria. Domine.

Offeratory *she responds*
Omnipotens aeterna Deus of stars,
Let your light outline our souls,
Anoint this love in vitam aeternam.
Almighty. Almight.

Canon *all*
Water, stars, people sursum corda;
The flow, the shine and love—
For one night more dignum et justam est.

they enter waters

36

By Any Other Name

Summer nights flowed like swamps in storm
There were new squeeks in the old mattress

Sex was the rhythm we played as night hatched
insects clung to leaves and branches and clothes

lines to wail for love their one and only
chance to search the dark to mate and die

A simple scent tossed to black air
as mute soliloquies that lack the heart

of any Juliet but still the male cells
scream silent replies to urge to grope

without regret for death for life for death
while you and I pause for another breath

Invitations to Return

i.

We lie in bed listening to trees
laughing in the strong wind.
Their courage is beyond me.
On my tongue loafs a question
as brittle as a china plate,
but like the communion wafer
I swallow it without chewing
and drift into sleep.

ii.

The dreams echoed with dishes
falling through the ceiling
to the floor of our life.
A choir formed by the bed,
silent, except for the soft noise
of robes falling from shoulders
to oblivion, and the harmony
flesh made as it lit the dark.

iii.

I woke standing at the window
and could taste stale bread
as I heard the hootin' & howlin'
of trees searching for the note
that would shatter the white moon
while you smiled in your dream
and reached a pale arm out
to where I was.

iii. the opening absence

My eyes gaze uncomprehendingly
at the space before me, and
I have an inkling of the neverendingness
of which I am the beginning.
——Paul Gauguin,
THE WRITINGS OF A SAVAGE

1

Night's emptiness lulls.
Time's calculations withdraw.
The mind promises itself
to what elements there are:

rain and wind, a tree,
the streetlamp,
which unites them
to the eye

These are small worlds
in the one world.

Speak some words
and the distance between us
closes.

2

Night encloses
as it opens.

Daylight had left a trail
of statements
no longer of use. True,
that primitives
horded gold in stone carved rooms,
prayed to gold
in the dark corners of rooms,
and spilled blood in lust
of afterlives,
in sun-longings,

but this streetlamp lights up
its brief pool,
its own golden globe in the nether
of a rain shortened
world, the only world left
to worship.

Listen,
the streetlamp
sings its own praises
while it can.

3

The tree seems lost,
arms stretched out,
fondling wind:

O rapture, O world,
take me where you will.
Here is never enough.

Wind shivers the leaves,
and they in turn
chatter and sparkle
in the lamp's breath, certain
that more will come,

that the journey names
its own destiny.

4

Rain laughs at heights.
The sound of rain laughing
is a hymn repeating itself
in the one journey foretold.

Each drop, falling,
shares one name,
is a family of common sorrows,

but the descent in darkness
leaves each orphaned,

leaves each falling
to private ordeals:

the leaf's empty, expectant palm,
the taut disharmony of telephone lines,
light suddenly blossoming into
the prism of blank droplets,
like faces in windows
lit by lightening.

These are brief, reckless joys,
and the last measure
of the fall
is spent desire.

5

Wind casts light to the tree,
generous and charitable
as an ancient father,

then slides wings of light
along its own back,

languishes, like this,

in the sensuous cool of rain
and the airy pool
of the only warmth,

only to imagine
beginning again.

It is no use to tempt further.
Even wind knows
pleasure's demise.

And the body cannot long
suffer ecstacy.

And always, wind desires
distance.

6

A sudden shift of horizon
and light softens.
The edges of its pool
contract. Night
grays. The place
wearies of itself.
Only the white center
refuses change.

Only the lamp, like a prophet
proved true, must go blind.
It is written, written here,
and wind and rain seek
the places of memory,
and the tree relearns its quiet,
and the only justice is choosing
which promise to break.

7

Looking back across
the opening absence,
as we must, are driven to
by the thing that
names us human,

we blink fraternity
to night's loss,
to sweated ecstacies
scattered in winds,
to the self offered to spaces

between light and dark, warmth
and cold, wet and dry, here
and there, until
bits of us
are irretrievable.

8

When fragments return,

in dream, the shapes of cloud,
the fogged paths of woods,
the songs of children,

the telling
is never the same,
with colors all wrong,
and the timing off.

Yet we listen and speech
fills with new promises:

This, too, is a passing.
The sun nears. Twist and turn
and open to another flow.

A NOTE ABOUT PRODUCTION

Type is hand set 10 point Old Colony Bold with 18 point Old Colony titles, originally designed by Frederic W. Goudy for use, along with his more famous Kennerley type, at his own Village Press, which he first established in 1903 in Park Ridge, Illinois. This book was letterpress printed at the Adastra Press on a hand feed, antique Pearl treadle press, in an edition of 400. The signatures were sewn by hand and bound in Strathmore Americana Williamsburg Blue paper, with 50 copies in boards, of which 25 have been signed and numbered by the author. Cover design is linoleum block cut.

ABOUT THE AUTHOR

GARY METRAS was born in Chicopee, Massachusetts, in 1947. He received a B. A. from the University of Massachusetts-Amherst and an M. A. from Goddard College. His poetry has appeared widely in small press magazines and in four previous pamphlets, the most recent being *The Yearnings* (Samisdat, 1980) and *The Necessities* (Adastra, 1979). An English teacher in a rural high school for the past several years, he has also worked as store clerk, short order cook, laborer, air traffic controller (U. S. Air Force, 1966–1970) and book store manager. He lives with his wife, Natalie, and children, Jason and Nadia, in Easthampton, Massachusetts.